PHOTOGRAPHING
Navajos

PHOTOGRAPHING
Navajos

John Collier Jr.
on the Reservation, 1948–1953

by
C. Stewart Doty
Dale Sperry Mudge
Herbert John Benally

Photographs by John Collier Jr.

UNIVERSITY OF NEW MEXICO PRESS · ALBUQUERQUE

Library of Congress Cataloging-in-Publication Data

Doty, C. Stewart, (Charles Stewart)

Photographing Navajos : John Collier Jr. on the reservation, 1948–1953 /

by C. Stewart Doty, Dale Sperry Mudge, Herbert J. Benally ;

photographs by John Collier Jr.

p. cm.

Includes bibliographical references.

ISBN 0-8263-2438-X (cloth)

1. Navajo Indians—Pictorial works.   2. Collier, John, 1913–

I. Mudge, Dale S., 1948–   .   II. Benally, Herbert J., 1944–   .

III. Collier, John, 1913–   .   IV. Title.

E99.N3D66 2002

979.1004'972—dc21

2002002303

This book is dedicated to

Alexander H. Leighton & Jane M. Murphy

Contents

Introduction
and Acknowledgments

THIS BOOK HAS AN interesting history. Two of its authors independently did work on French-speaking Acadians in northern Maine. University of Maine Professor Emeritus of History C. Stewart Doty published *Acadian Hard Times: The Farm Security Administration in Maine's St. John Valley, 1940–1943* (1991), which combined historic photographs by John Collier Jr. with documentation from the National Archives and interviews with photographed family members. Independent scholar Dale S. Mudge produced and directed *True North-Acadian Yarns* (1997), a documentary for Maine Public Television, and a scholarly article based on her interviews with Acadian women handcrafters who knitted and crocheted for pay during the Great Depression.

Before he met Mudge, Doty had learned from a University of Maine colleague that John Collier Jr. had also photographed Nova Scotia Acadians. Thinking that the Maine and Nova Scotia Acadian photographs might make an interesting comparative study, Doty eventually located the photographs in the Public Archives of Nova Scotia. The project did not work out, however, and Doty relocated to New Mexico.

Mudge and Doty finally met in 1999. He suggested that she do the comparative study of Acadians, and gave her the finding aid to the Nova Scotia photographs, which also listed over three hundred Collier photographs of Navajos. Mudge drove from Maine to Halifax to look at them. But Mudge's background in farming, sheep raising, and weaving made her more interested in the Navajo photographs, so they decided to collaborate on this project instead.

By 2000 Mudge and Doty obtained permission to use the photographs from their custodian, Alexander H. Leighton. At the University of Pennsylvania, Mudge found another collection of Navajo photographs, which Collier had taken in 1948 for *Farm Quarterly*. In turn, the Leightons found several hundred more Collier photographic negatives in the attic of their Nova Scotia home. Nova Scotia and Pennsylvania were unlikely places to find Collier photographs of Navajos, but there they were.

Mudge and Doty felt comfortable working with their Acadian fellow citizens of Maine, but they believed that they needed a Navajo collaborator for a work on Collier's Navajo photographs. Doty met with Diné College instructor in Navajo History and Culture, Herbert J. Benally, who had published on Navajo culture and the Navajo way of knowing. Benally agreed to join the project. The three authors then secured a grant from the New Mexico Endowment for the Humanities to fund research and photograph production for a book and museum exhibition. In 2001 Mudge spent several months interviewing surviving family members of Collier's Fruitland photographic subjects. This book is the result of the collaboration of the three authors. It coincides with the opening of an exhibition of the same title at The Albuquerque Museum.

The support of the New Mexico Endowment for the Humanities and the advice of its program director, Wade Patterson, made this book and exhibition possible. The authors especially thank Alexander H. Leighton, Jane P. Murphy, Mary Collier, and Malcolm Collier for their generous advice and counsel; Ellen Landis of The Albuquerque Museum for setting them on the right path to create the museum exhibition; Lois Yorke and her staff at the Public Archives of Nova Scotia; and staff at the University of Pennsylvania for providing images for the project.

C. Stewart Doty also thanks the librarians at the Zimmerman Library of the University of New Mexico, the Albuquerque Public Library, and the Huntington Library in San Marino, California. He especially thanks reference librarian Mel Johnson of the Fogler Library of the University of Maine for locating, as usual, the unlocatable.

Dale S. Mudge spent over four months locating and interviewing the Navajo people in Collier's photographs. This work would never have been possible without the generous contribution of time and effort of Joanne Benally, Nancy Lawrence, and Maxine Davis. They helped her navigate the back roads on the reservation and spent countless hours making contact with the subjects in the photographs. They interpreted hours of interviews and explained many Navajo customs and traditions to help Mudge understand Navajo culture. Their insight and appreciation for the photographs were rewarding and their tireless assistance helped accomplish the work that needed to be done. Mudge is deeply gratified to have their friendship, understanding, and professional help. The families Dale Mudge interviewed were so generous with their time, explaining the content of the photographs and their family histories. She especially thanks Richard Golbe, Leroy Duncan, Guy Greyhorse, Lorriane Sam, and Ethel and Ruben Yazzie for explaining the details of the photographs, sharing their insight into farming fifty years ago, and for their deep appreciation of preserving this historical record.

Mudge also thanks the following people for all the information they provided within the Navajo community and for their encouraging interest and help: Karen and Timothy Benally, Elaine Benally, Wade Davies, Peter and Marlene Kakos, Shirley Lowe, Irene Nez, and Janet Turnbull.

Mudge's work would also never have proceeded without the enormous help of Charliene Barns. She introduced Mudge to Farmington residents who could help her understand the oil and gas industry. Bob Bayless and Tom Duggan gave much of their time to explain the economic development of the San Juan basin.

Herbert J. Benally wishes to thank Lillie Peteman for helping him understand the cultural context of the period in which the Collier photographs were taken and also to extend gratitude to Judith Ellen Osborn for her readings and suggestions for clarity for the non-Navajo audience.

The John Collier Jr. and Mary Collier family will give their archive to the Maxwell Museum of Anthropology. The collection includes fifty years of photographs, film and video, field notes, daybooks, and correspondence. The intention of the family is to make the images accessible to members of the communities involved as well as to scholars and students in art, photography, and anthropology. The Collier Family collection will be housed in the Maxwell Museum.

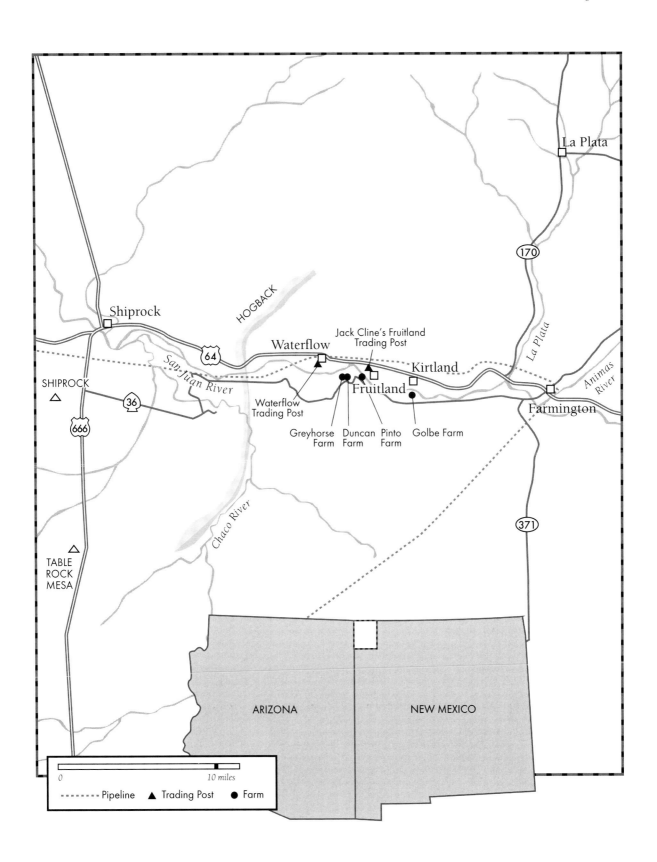

Introduction

John Collier Jr.'s
Photographs of Navajos
Breaking New Ground

By Herbert John Benally

JOHN COLLIER JR.'S PHOTOGRAPHS give us a window through which to view segments of Navajo culture and spirituality as they were in the late 1940s and early 1950s. Photographs do not speak for themselves, but by combining particular photographs with additional knowledge we can better understand the Navajo life of the past. The original name of the Navajo is "Diné," meaning "the people." The word Navajo, according to Spanish record, is a Tewa term meaning "People of the Great Planted Fields." To understand the people in the photographs, one must understand how they came to be in their current location and economic situation. The 1940s and 1950s were turbulent times for the Navajo. In these two decades the Navajo experienced major assaults on their way of life by the federal government through forced livestock reduction, religious persecution by Christians and assimilationists, and by World War II.

Collier's photos exemplify people restoring a life in the wake of turmoil. The photographs depict people reduced to poverty, breaking new ground for the future after having their core shaken. The relocation of Navajos to farmland signified an attempt to correct a federal government fiasco. For some of these relocatees the only choice was to leave behind their relatives and homes and move away. Anxiety, nervousness, and trepidation are apparent on the faces of these people whose world had been turned upside down. On the lighter side, 1950 was the beginning of a new era in Navajo development. The thousands of servicemen and munitions workers who returned to the Reservation gained experience in wage economy and were aware of the importance of formal Western education. Severe poverty and hardship continued, however, until the establishment of the Office of Economic Opportunity during the John F. Kennedy administration.

The Creation

Shiprock is the home of the mythological creature Monster Bird. It is also the site where the culture heroes Monster Slayer and Child of Water slew the man-eating Monster Bird. In Navajo creation stories, culture and land are integrally connected. The origin of the Navajo lies in the Black World. It is here that First Man and First Woman came into existence. The primal couple, Coyote, and insect beings cultivated fields, built homes, and formed a government. The group, some say, practiced black magic, engaged in illicit sexual activities, corrupted their government, and began to fight with one another. For these reasons the Creators drove them from the First World.

The group emerged in the Second World, the Blue World, where they met other beings. After a brief violent encounter with these beings, the newcomers established peace with them. This world was barren. For unknown reasons suffering and sorrow caused the beings to migrate to the Third World, the Yellow World. Here they found themselves in the midst of six mountains and two great rivers that crossed each other. This world was also inhabited by other beings.

One day Coyote observed First Man taking an inventory of the paraphernalia in his medicine bundle. Coyote asked First Man for a piece of the white shell that fell from the medicine bundle.

Fig. 1

The mesa south and west of Fruitland, with Shiprock in the distance.

Courtesy of Nova Scotia Archives.

First Man denied his request three times before giving Coyote a sacred white shell. Once this power came into the Coyote's possession, he took it to where the water people lived. With the white shell he created a tide and a baby water monster washed ashore. Coyote took the baby and in four days it started to rain. The water rose until only the tips of the mountains were visible. The beings led by First Man huddled on the eastern sacred mountain. There they planted various trees to see if any of them would grow tall enough to reach the sky. As a last resort, First Man planted a female reed and this giant reed grew until it reached the sky. First Man and the beings made an opening and ascended into the Fourth World, the Glittering World.

First Man and other beings proceeded to recreate the formless New World. The Holy People entered the newly created world and became its inner spirit. It is with this understanding that Navajo refer to the earth as their Mother. The earth is a living entity capable of thought, feeling, movement, and speech. Consequently, this knowledge and belief govern our behavior and thought toward creation.

First Man collected soil from the six mountains of the Third World and replanted it in the Fourth World. He endowed each mountain with thought, livelihood, life, and fulfillment. Whenever we use the resources from these mountains today, we tap into those primal endowments, which manifest in our lives as wisdom, knowledge, livelihood, living, and contentment in old age. The mountains are also the land boundaries of the Navajo people. The elders say that if one were to place a light on the summit of each of the four major mountains and tilt each light at forty-five degrees, all the rays would meet in the sky above the center of the Navajo homeland. When these invisible rays (poles) are draped with a rainbow, they form what we know as the male hogan.

According to Navajo creation stories, when Coyote overheard the creators discussing reorganizing the world, he counseled them that organization without first planning for a home was fruitless. Hence, Talking God instructed First Man and Woman how to build their home. When he visited the couple at their dwelling, he found trash scattered in and around the hogan, the bed not made, the dishes not washed, and the floor not swept. He said to the woman, "My grandchild, I want to say a few things to you about the home. The unkempt bed, the unswept floor, and the dirty dishes all lead to poverty and hardship." Inside the home were some valuables hanging on the wall. He pointed to them and said, "If you want to keep and increase your valuables then you must pick up the trash, sweep the floor, and wash the dishes. The organized way of life leads to greater order, prosperity, and happiness." These teachings have been passed on from generation to generation.

Traditional Navajo Culture
and Daily Life

The Home

The Navajo worldview is dualistic; the universe is a complementary female and male phenomenon. For this reason, beside the male hogan stands a female hogan. The two types of hogans are still in use today. The male hogan is shaped like a teepee, while the female hogan's prominent features are its circular wall and earth-covered dome-shaped roof of timber cribbing with a central smoke hole. Modern variations of the female hogan include hexagonal frame houses, circular log cabin–type structures with circular stone walls and earthen roofs. Traditionally the entrances of both structures face east to welcome the Gods as they arrive with the dawn to bestow blessings.

The interior space of the hogan is divided between the husband and wife. The woman's domain in the hogan is on the north side, where her kitchen and loom for weaving are located. The couple's bedding is located in the west directly behind the centrally located stove. The man's domain is on the south side where his saddle, ax, tools, and woodpile are found. In a one-room dwelling, space is

Fig. 2

A tee-pee–shaped male hogan.

Courtesy of Alexander H. Leighton.

Fig. 3

The Fruitland Project anthropologists followed Alexander Leighton's method of making an inventory of housing. One of John Collier Jr.'s assignments was to take images like this of Fruitland Navajo housing.

Courtesy of Nova Scotia Archives.

Fig. 4

A meal of fry bread and coffee in a hogan. The meal and background show the material culture of 1948 Navajos.

Courtesy of University of Pennsylvania Museum, Philadelphia (neg. #54-143963).

versatile. For example, as soon as the family arises the beds are taken out to air and the room is swept and breakfast is served. Then the utensils are cleared and the room becomes a workspace. Because the dwelling lacks shelves, items such as letters, pictures, playing cards, cigarettes, herbs, and the medicine bundle are hung on nails.

A prominent feature of a home is a shade house. The summers are hot and a shade house is a necessity. This is where the family will cook, sleep, and work during the summer. Another common object is a cross beam where the family bedding is aired out daily. A wagon containing a barrel is also a common sight since the family water supply is obtained from a well or a spring that is distant from the home. When the family cannot afford a wagon, water is hand-carried in buckets from as far away as two miles. Even today, in 2002, some families still haul water in pickup trucks for domestic use.

Meals

Fried potatoes with tortillas and coffee were commonly served three times a day. This basic diet was supplemented with farm produce, goat milk, and mutton when available. The goats were milked in the morning and late afternoon. Children drank the milk as it came from the goats and the elders boiled it and enjoyed it with tortillas and coffee. When the family could afford it, Spam and onions were added to the fried potatoes. Contrary to popular belief, fry bread with coffee was served only occasionally, and it was a treat. During the fifties the Navajo did not eat much mutton either; it was saved for special occasions and supplemented their meager food supplies. Children would eagerly look forward to the butchering of a sheep, as one would anticipate a Christmas dinner. The liver, intestines, stomach, and ribs were delicacies. Even today Navajos still crave these things.

Lively discussions and humor accompanied meals. Everyone ate from the same bowl or plate as

Fig. 5

Cooking fry bread in a hogan.

Courtesy of University of Pennsylvania Museum, Philadelphia (neg. #54-143967).

Fig. 6

A Navajo woman milking one of the family goats. Edited 1948 Collier Navajo Mountain, Utah image.

Courtesy of University of Pennsylvania Museum, Philadelphia (neg. #54.143954).

was the custom. Grace was given at the end of the meal when people would pat themselves with their hands while saying a prayer, "Thank you for a fine meal, that it will give us strength and that we may continue to walk in beauty."

Clans

According to sacred stories, the goddess Changing Woman created the four original Navajo clans. These clans have since divided many times. Navajos have adopted other people, such as former war captives or people from other tribes who chose to live with them. Today, descendents of these people are members of the Navajo Tribe.

Children

In Navajo philosophy wealth is measured in number of children. The children are the strength of the parents and the might of old age. K'é is a concept that expresses terms of endearment. A new mother embraces her new infant with the words "she'awéé shiyáazhí" (my baby, my little one). These terms of endearment for bonding never diminish but grow in intensity with time. Traditionally children were taught to use kinship terms when they addressed relatives. The use of personal names was not approved for it was disrespectful to call someone by name. Kinship relationship terms communicate and reinforce an acceptance, belonging, and caring to the person to whom they are directed.

Selecting a child's name was also was important, for a child grows to fill that name. A person may have three names: a sacred name, which is only divulged in a ceremonial setting; a community name given to him by the community members; and an English name. The community name may refer to a person's physical characteristics, attitude, possessions, place of residence, or clan affiliation and may not be one that a person would select for himself. "The Man Who Plucks His Mustache" and "Skinny

Fig. 7

Collier showed this 1948 photograph to a Fruitland Navajo in 1952–1953 who explained, "The colors are black, brown, and yellow. Made of long haired wool. It's smooth. The mother's spinning. You can see it's long haired wool. Daughter weaving. Sometimes they make a rug together. Look at the goods and clothes. They're much richer than other families."

Courtesy of Nova Scotia Archives.

Woman" are good examples. Navajos of the early fifties always faced a dilemma when asked for their names. Should they give the sacred name or the community name? Sometimes a person would ask his neighbor to announce his community name. Some would say they had no name; in such cases a trader, teacher, or a missionary would give the person a name. Such names as Brigham Young, Calvin Coolidge, and John Smith were a result of that practice.

Hair

The Navajo believe that a person's hair is sacred and that the body is a microcosm of the universe. A person's head extends into heaven and is crowned with hair that represents the male and female rain. We know that water brings creation to fruition. Hair is also symbolically associated with thought. Thought is considered to be similar to water, for thought gives rise to life, growth, and prosperity. The first time a child's hair was cut, that hair was ceremonially burned. Thereafter, hair yielded from cutting or combing was collected and burned to prevent sacrilege. Hair neatly tied indicated a spiritually organized life.

Most of the Navajo women in the Collier photographs wear their hair in the traditional style. Always practical, the federal boarding schools cut the girls' hair to prevent lice. "We cried when our long beautiful hair was cut," remembered a woman of her school days. The girls in the photos all have their hair braided. This is a good example of a culture in transition. Traditional Navajo hair was never braided.

Dressing for the Trading Post

The woman would dress in her velvet blouse with silver buttons, turquoise necklace, flowing skirts, and Pendleton shawl, and her man, in his cowboy boots and hat, would hitch a wagon and head for

Fig. 8

Girls in the Navajo Mountain Community School dressing their hair after washing. Most Navajo have to haul every drop of water they use for many miles, so bathing is at a minimum. But, when they can have water, they are ardent bathers. They are very proud of their fine black hair and wash it out whenever they get an opportunity. Collier caption.

Courtesy of University of Pennsylvania Museum, Philadelphia (neg. #54-143952).

the nearest trading post. The trading post was the social center of the community. It was here that the couple caught up with the community news.

Work

Learning to work was also important. Traditionally, the work of a man lay outside and the woman's responsibilities lay inside and around the home. These are the general rules for distinguishing between the roles and responsibilities of a boy and girl. For instance, the boys were instructed to care for the animals, chop firewood, and haul water. The girls were taught organization skills and knowledge associated with the home, weaving, caring for livestock, cooking, and child rearing. The children were told if they worked hard, their minds and bodies would become strong. "Elders would advise parents to 'teach the children while they are yet tender and when their minds can still be bent and shaped like a young willow' and remind them that 'It is hard when their minds have formed. Instill in them appropriate habits and they will discover reasons for their behavior when they come of age.'"[1]

Farming

Farming is not new to the Navajo. It is something they have done from time immemorial. For instance, in 1582 Spanish explorer Antonio de Espejo recorded, "We found here peaceful Indian mountaineers who brought us tortillas even though we did not need them."[2] Moreover, Acrey stated that Espejo and his men encountered more Navajos south of Mt. Taylor where he and his men burned shacks and destroyed a maize (corn) field.[3] Farming did not stop with the introduction of sheep; families have always kept a small farm for themselves, but very little of the produce was grown for commercial use. Hence, farming for the market was a new venture for those Navajos who were relocated along the San Juan River in the 1950s.

Fig. 9

Many Fruitland Navajos make pilgrimages to their original home places,
either high in the mountains or in isolated arid deserts. Edited Collier caption.

Courtesy of Nova Scotia Archives.

Fig. 10

Spring plowing in the irrigated fields.

Courtesy of Nova Scotia Archives.

Background History for
Understanding Collier Photographs

To interpret John Collier Jr.'s photographs it is necessary to have some understanding of Navajo history that preceded them. In 1863 the Navajo people were captured and marched from their homeland to imprisonment at Bosque Redondo in eastern New Mexico. Following their release and the signing of a treaty in 1868, they were permitted to return to what formerly was their ancient land, but was now federal land that was held in trust for them. In accordance with this treaty Navajos became landless in their own country. The treaty land that they were permitted to reside on existed at the whim of the federal government.

In this treaty the federal government agreed to allot sheep to the Navajos. They were given two sheep each, and many people literally starved themselves and their children to increase the size of their herds to meet their future needs. Due to their sacrifice, from 1868 to 1933 the sheep and goats had multiplied into well over a million. A number of studies and reports between 1883 and 1933 claimed that it might become necessary to limit the size of Navajo herds because the reservation had more animals than it could conceivably support. The overgrazing of the high plains desert land of the Navajo reservation resulted in severe soil erosion.

Meanwhile, to the west of the Navajo reservation, a giant structure called Boulder Dam was being constructed. At a glance these two developments do not appear to be related, but in fact strong political and environmental connections did exist. It was apparent to the soil conservationists of the time that silt originating from the soil erosion on the Navajo reservation posed a threat to the dam. Commenting on the importance of the dam, Richard White asserted, "The dam both protected the Imperial Valley of California and made possible a greatly improved irrigation system. It also guaranteed water to Los Angeles and southern California; as an added benefit, it generated enough electricity to supply the

Fig. 11

Navajo women driving sheep on the road for sale at Jack Cline's Fruitland Trading Post.

Courtesy of Alexander H. Leighton.

entire Southwest."[4] Consequently, the building of Boulder Dam increased the urgency for remedying Navajo land erosion caused by overgrazing. The task of restoring balance to the environment fell on John Collier, the father of the photographer John Collier Jr. When Collier, a long-time advocate of cultural pluralism, became Commissioner of Indian Affairs in 1933, he believed in Indian cultural survival and self-determination and was bent on reversing the federal government's Indian assimilation policy.

This is not what the Navajo remember Collier for, however. They remember him for his role in the slaughtering of Navajo sheep, goats, and horses and placing the people in poverty. Collier spearheaded the infamous stock reduction program as the way to remedy land erosion through overgrazing. He initially attempted to persuade Navajos to exercise range management and to voluntarily reduce the number of animals on the range.

To persuade Navajos to voluntarily reduce their stock, Collier offered several recommendations. One recommendation was that "Compensation for livestock losses would come from both the federal government, who would finance the purchase of the livestock, and from wages paid to those Navajos who work on government programs on the reservation."[5] But this recommendation would come to have unfortunate consequences. Many people who sold livestock went to work for the Civilian Conservation Corps (CCC), but "Relief work, which under Collier's original plan was meant only to be an expedient to tide the Navajos over until the range was restored (a process then presumed to take four or five years), had become a mainstay of the Navajo economy. Planners clearly recognized the implications. Since the termination of the work projects would 'seriously affect the Navajo level of subsistence,' a new source of income must be found."[6]

Finally, a forced livestock reduction was imposed in 1933. Collier successfully persuaded the Navajo Tribal Council to support livestock reduction by selling 100,000 sheep and goats. The first round of stock reduction went well. The second phase of the program called for a reduction of 150,000 goats and 50,000 sheep. It was during the second stock reduction that things got out of hand. The weather was bad the day the animals were to be gathered for shipping. Orders were given to those in the field to destroy the animals after they were purchased. Many animals were driven into washes and canyons, and then shot and burned. To complete the reduction quota the government employees were ordered to go to Navajo homes and enter the corrals, shoot half of the animals, and move on to the next homes. "The persistent Navajo question, 'If you take our stock, how shall we live?' deserved an answer. The bureau's own data indicated that its response so far had been glib and unrealistic."[7]

The impact of the stock reduction on the psychology of the Navajo life was incredible. As Mary Jumbo's mother-in-law later recalled, "We were so scared. Everybody was bossin'. It is hard to tell who it was. Maybe it was a common Indian tellin' us we had to do a certain thing. And we did it. We were so scared of everything."[8] Another elder lamented, "All was going well, and the people had increased their livestock very rapidly, when along came John Collier and stomped his big foot on our sheep, goats and horses—and crushed them before our eyes. We believe that is when the rain went with the sheep. If it hadn't happened we would have rain and green ranges with sheep grazing all over."[9] The Navajos' objection to the stock reduction fell on deaf ears and they understood how powerless they were in their relationship with the U.S. government.

According to White, "The Navajos reacted to the insecurity and suffering which goat reduction brought both by moving into opposition to the New Deal and John Collier and by increasing the number of ceremonies in order to restore balance to a world seemingly dissolving into chaos."[10] Clyde Kluckhohn's studies in Ramah, New Mexico revealed that "Navajo men devoted one-fourth to one-third of their productive time to ceremonials and women one-fifth to one-third of theirs and that the percentage had probably been higher in the recent past."[11] An elder added, "It all added up to hardship and distress for many years for the Navajos, right down to the present generation. Even some of our own habits and products seem to have vanished. Many times I think about this as I work among the people and as I travel to different places."[12]

In the face of a growing sense of powerlessness and increasing poverty the Navajos turned to the Native American Church (NAC) and its ceremonial use of peyote. NAC offered the people a way to cope with a world that had been profoundly disturbed by the federal government. The tribal leader, Jacob Morgan, contested the adoption of this new religion. In 1940 he introduced before the Tribal Council a resolution prohibiting NAC on the reservation, and the resolution passed. But when it came to enforcing the resolution, John Collier informed the tribe that it was a tribal law and the federal government would not become involved in the exercising of tribal sovereignty. During World War II soldiers' families would assemble and conduct NAC prayer meetings. The police would raid the ceremony, arrest the priest, and confiscate the paraphernalia. It was not until 1967 via another Navajo Tribal Council resolution that NAC members were legally permitted to practice their beliefs and transport peyote on the reservation.

In Washington, D.C., John Collier also pushed the passage of the Wheeler-Howard Indian Reorganization Act (IRA), a program that counteracted the destructive features of the Dawes Severalty Act of 1887, which had tried to assimilate and acculturate Native Americans into mainstream American culture. The Dawes Act had been among the most damaging legislation regarding Native Americans. It had severed families, disrupted traditional education, broken up reservation land, and promoted paternalistic relationships between native tribes and the federal government.

During World War II many Navajos joined the various branches of the armed services; others found employment in munitions depots in Flagstaff and Winslow, Arizona. When the war ended in 1945, thousands of Navajo servicemen and munitions workers returned to the reservation, bringing knowledge of a wage-based economy. They returned to a home that had drastically changed. The

Fig. 12

A medicine man surveying his paraphernalia.

Courtesy of Alexander H. Leighton.

pastoral economy, the major source of subsistence prior to the stock reduction, had become a thing of the past. Therefore, they had to seek wage work; however, on the reservation there were no jobs available. This was the situation when John Collier Jr. arrived in Upper Fruitland to photograph.

Notes

1. Herbert J. Benally, "Spiritual Knowledge for a Secular Society," *Journal of American Indian Higher Education* 4 (1992): 20.
2. Bill P. Acrey, *Navajo History: The Land and the People* (Shiprock, N.Mex.: Central Consolidated School District Number 22, 1988), 46.
3. Ibid., 47.
4. Richard White, *The Roots of Dependency* (Lincoln: University of Nebraska Press, 1983), 251.
5. Acrey, *Navajo History,* 233.
6. White, *Roots of Dependency,* 282.
7. Ibid.
8. Ibid., 264.
9. Broderick H. Johnson, *Stories of Traditional Navajo Life and Culture* (Tsaile, Ariz.: Navajo Community College Press, 1977), 161.
10. White, *Roots of Dependency,* 267.
11. Ibid.
12. Johnson, *Stories of Traditional Navajo Life and Culture,* 144.

Select Bibliography

Aberle, David F. *The Peyote Religion Among the Navaho,* 2d ed. Norman: University of Oklahoma Press, 1982.

Bailey, L. R. *The Long Walk: A History of the Navajo Wars, 1846–1868.* Pasadena: Socio-Technical Books, 1970.

Bigham, Sam and Janet. *Between Sacred Mountains.* Chinle, Ariz.: Rock Point Community School, 1983.

Boyce, George A. *When Navajos Had Too Many Sheep: The 1940s.* San Francisco: Indian Historian Press, 1974.

Iverson, Peter. *The Navajo Nation.* Albuquerque: University of New Mexico Press, 1984.

Johnson, Broderick and Ruth Roessel, eds. *The People: A Study of the Navajos.* Lawrence, Kans.: Haskell Print Shop, 1948.

Locke, Raymond Friday. *The Book of the Navajo.* Los Angeles: Mankind Publishing Co., 1992.

Portfolio: 1948 Collier Photographs of Navajos

IN 1948 JOHN COLLIER JR. had taken photographs of Arizona Navajos for an article in *Farm Quarterly*. These images are from that photographic assignment. When he joined the Fruitland project in 1952, Collier created a portfolio of *Farm Quarterly* images to show Fruitland Navajos and elicit their responses. "We chose a wide assortment of photographs," Collier later wrote, "and assembled an interview file that was designed to gather statements on Navajo life values—general values, not personal statements about personal lives."

"We found that Navajos," Collier added, "being a nature oriented people and still having to make many decisions from direct observation of environment, were in every way better observers. . . . The Indians were far more fluid in their photographic reading, giving identification and explanation of fine detail, and being able to state with great accuracy place, season, date and even time of day of a large number of photographs."

The captions for the following images use those responses to Collier and the anthropological team.

Fig. 13

A Navajo girl.

Courtesy of University of Pennsylvania Museum, Philadelphia (neg. #54-143969).

Fig. 14

Wagons are the most common means of transportation in Navajo country. Horses and wagons can always get over the rugged trails that connect the isolated Navajo camps with the few main roads. Collier caption for a 1948 Chinle Valley, Arizona image.

Courtesy of University of Pennsylvania Museum, Philadelphia (neg. #54-143962).

Fig 15

After the noon meal, a Navajo family and relatives relax upon sheep skins around the hogan fire.
Edited Collier caption of 1948 Burnt Corn Valley, Arizona image.

Courtesy of University of Pennsylvania Museum, Philadelphia (neg. #54-143965).

Fig. 16

A Navajo family and their hogan at Navajo Mountain, Utah.

Courtesy of University of Pennsylvania Museum, Philadelphia (neg. #54-143959).

Fig. 17

On the left is a medicine man, working on a sandpainting of the
Four Wind People near Ganado, Arizona. Edited Collier caption.

Courtesy of University of Pennsylvania Museum, Philadelphia (neg. #54-143957).

Fig. 18

Sheep shearing time. Just as soon as the chill is gone from the nights, the Navajos shear their sheep. The sale of wool often brings them the first hard cash they have seen all winter. They pay up as many bills as they can and then get by until fall when they sell their lambs. Collier caption for a Navajo Mountain, Utah image.

Courtesy of University of Pennsylvania Museum, Philadelphia (neg. #54-143955).

Fig. 19

In the summer, the Navajo women set up their looms out of doors, but through icy months of the winter all weaving is done inside the hogan. Collier caption for his 1948 Burnt Corn Valley, Arizona image.

Courtesy of University of Pennsylvania Museum, Philadelphia (neg. #54-143970).

Fig. 20

Hogan at the foot of Navajo Mountain, one of the four sacred mountains of the Navajos. Collier caption.

Courtesy of University of Pennsylvania Museum, Philadelphia (neg. #54-143961).

Fig. 21

Hogans of a Navajo farmer and medicine man at Moencopi Wash, near Tuba City, Arizona. Edited Collier caption.

Courtesy of University of Pennsylvania Museum, Philadelphia (neg. #54-143953).

Fig. 22

A skilled Navajo weaver, who lives near Wide Ruins, Arizona. Edited Collier caption.

Courtesy of University of Pennsylvania Museum, Philadelphia (neg. #54-143968).

Fig. 23

A Navajo farmer cultivated with his homemade cultivator that the Indians designed to loosen the hard top soil without exposing the field to serious evaporation and wind erosion. A shallow blade cuts three or four inches below the surface, opening the soil for irrigation and removing any stray weeds. Edited Collier caption of 1948 Moencopi Wash image.

Courtesy of University of Pennsylvania Museum, Philadelphia (neg. #54-143958).

Fig. 24

"Look," a Fruitland Navajo handed this *Farm Quarterly* image to her daughter. "Her own lamb. She's raising it herself. It's all her own." "Will her father sell it when it's grown?" "No, never, without the girl's permission," replied the daughter. "It's hers, and all its lambs will be hers. She will own them, even when they are a big herd."

Courtesy of Nova Scotia Archives.

Fig. 25

A close up of sheep shearing.

Courtesy of University of Pennsylvania Museum, Philadelphia (neg. #54-143966).

Fig. 26

Getting ready to shell corn.

Courtesy of University of Pennsylvania Museum, Philadelphia (neg. #54-143964).

The trading post at Piñon, Arizona, in the north central part of the Navajo Reservation. The trading post is the center of the Navajo's commercial life. Here, he sells his produce and establishes credit. The trader is his banker and often his counselor in the complicated ways of the white man. Collier caption.

Courtesy of University of Pennsylvania Museum, Philadelphia (neg. #54-143956).

Fig. 28

When a Navajo goes to the trading post to trade, he usually loads his wagon with water casks. Every drop of water must be hauled to the isolated Navajo hogans. Collier caption.

Courtesy of University of Pennsylvania Museum, Philadelphia (neg. #54-143960).

Fig. 29

"This field has been marked and planted," a Fruitland Navajo said of this Collier photograph taken earlier of Arizona Navajos. "Now they are irrigating. Yes, the women do a lot of the farming, irrigating, planting, and gathering. Yes, more than the old days. The men are away working now."

Courtesy of Nova Scotia Archives.

Fig. 30

Collier described this image as traditional style cooking in the mountains west of the San Juan basin, where many Fruitland settlers originally lived.

Courtesy of Nova Scotia Archives.

Fig. 31

A Fruitland Navajo said this about this photograph of Arizona Navajos, "No, the family is not lonely. There must be other hogans just beyond the picture, maybe two or three. See the horse. In the old days we could go anywheres to see our friends. Winter or summer, we were never lonely. Now cars can't go up the mesas. They get stuck in the washes."

Courtesy of Nova Scotia Archives.

Fig. 32

Collier showed Fruitland Navajos photographs taken in other parts of the reservation. "Here is an old fashion family," said one Navajo viewer. "Long hair and head band. Uneducated family. Perhaps far away, for there are no hogans like that near Fruitland. Here is the whole family, grandfather, grandmother, son, daughter-in-law, children, and grandbabies. This is the way families used to stick together in the old days."

Courtesy of Nova Scotia Archives.

Fig. 33

Collier showed this 1948 *Farm Quarterly* photograph to a Fruitland Navajo and asked, "What could he be doing?"
The Fruitlander studied the picture in silence. "We just don't know what he's doing." Then the family talked
rapidly among themselves in Navajo. Later, one acculturated Navajo said, "He's a medicine man, of course. No,
he's not collecting pollen. He's collecting little black seeds to feed the ewes to make them have many lambs."

Courtesy of Nova Scotia Archives.

John Collier Jr.
Comes to Navajo Country

by C. Stewart Doty

IN THE SUMMER OF 1952 John Collier Jr. and his family pitched their tents in the cottonwood trees along the San Juan River behind the Fruitland Trading Post. Collier had come to New Mexico's Navajo country as a photographer for a Cornell University anthropology project. Sometimes his wife, Mary, would wash the photographic prints in the San Juan River. The project at Fruitland, led by anthropologist Tom T. Sasaki, had started in 1948 and continued until 1956. Its purpose was to examine the ways Navajo life was changing. In 1952 and again in 1953 Collier's job was to find "systematic ways of getting knowledge out of pictures" of Navajos for the team's anthropologists to use.[1] Nearly 1,000 Collier photographs still exist from this project. Until now, fewer than thirty-five of them have been published.[2] Yet at least two hundred of these images are among the finest photographs ever taken of the Navajo people. They show the shift from the traditional pastoral Navajo life of raising sheep and weaving wool to cash-crop agriculture, urban wage work, and a closer connection to the rest of the world.

John Collier Jr.'s (1913–1992) training and career made him particularly useful for the project's research. He was a member of an important family. His father, John Collier Sr., was an early advocate and activist for the rights of Native Americans. When John Jr. was eight years old, the family moved to Taos, New Mexico, to join other advocates for Native Americans such as author Mary Austin and cultural leader Mabel Dodge Luhan. They even spent their first night in Taos in the Luhan home.[3] In the 1920s John Collier Sr., Austin, and others worked to defeat the so-called Bursum Bill, which would have dispossessed Pueblo Indians of their lands. Collier Sr. and his colleagues also worked to improve the material conditions of Native Americans while preserving their distinctive cultures in the face of threatened assimilation.

This record led President Franklin D. Roosevelt to appoint John Collier Sr. Commissioner of the Bureau of Indian Affairs, and in this position he sought to make education and health care more accessible to the Navajo Nation. He substituted a policy of religious freedom for an earlier government policy opposed to native religious belief and ceremonies. He fought to replace the hated boarding schools with accessible day schools, but his plans could not be carried out until long after he left the Bureau. Convinced that reducing the number of sheep and goats would improve the Navajo economy and reduce soil erosion during the Dust Bowl days, Collier also put through a stock reduction program. Collier's Bureau of Indian Affairs cut in half Navajo herds of sheep and goats, the backbone of the Navajo economy and culture. Consequently, stock reduction and the name of John Collier Sr. are still hated by Navajo people.

John Collier Jr. started his life with some challenges. Injured as a child, he constantly struggled with learning disabilities and hearing loss. Because of these problems, his family directed him into the arts. As a teenager he apprenticed with California painter and muralist Maynard Dixon, and he developed a strong sense of design and landscape. In turn, photographer Dorothea Lange, Dixon's wife at the time, led Collier into photography. Working with her and in San Francisco photography laboratories, he learned both how to take pictures and how to develop and print his work.

In 1940 Collier shot photographs of Navajo sheep herding at Atarque, south of Ramah, and Zuni,

New Mexico. When Dorothea Lange saw them, she recommended him to Roy Stryker. In 1941 Collier joined Stryker's famous team of Farm Security Administration (FSA) photographers.[4] In taking pictures to document this New Deal agency's help to the rural poor, they also documented the lives of ordinary people. The work of the FSA photographers defined for most Americans the image of the Great Depression. Like other FSA photographers, Collier worked with 4 x 5 Speed Graphic, 35-mm Leica, and Rollei cameras. From the images he took, one can retrace his steps. Often he shot an image from the side of the road. For example, Collier took a quintessential landscape photograph of inland Maine by stopping at a roadside in Patton to photograph a potato field with Mount Katahdin in the background.

From the beginning of his work with the FSA photographic unit, Collier had trouble obeying the FSA rules, but he seemed to have a knack for connecting with his subjects. On his first trip to New England, Collier vividly described the autumn countryside and the farm markets. "These things I see with my eyes and feel with my emotions," he proclaimed.[5] He was especially proud of his FSA photographs of the Amish farmers in Lancaster County, Pennsylvania, French-speaking Acadian potato farmers and handcrafters in northern Maine, and the people of the New Mexico Hispanic communities in the high country between Taos and Santa Fe.

In fact, Collier created his most successful documentary work for the FSA in New Mexico in 1943. He wanted to try a photo essay of Taos Pueblo, and he went before the pueblo's council to get permission.[6] His motives in the shoot showed remarkable congruence with his father's program: "Contrary to the unfortunate example of democracy demonstrated by [its treatment of] the Negro, our administration of the Indian, to date, is a clean record. Under the present administration the Indians have benefited 100% under our democracy. Inherent in our Indians program is the benefit of the 'four freedoms'." As he explained it to Stryker, "I hope to do a community study, centering around the tribal self-government—Pictures of the council, its functions, and some left out stories of Indian families. If I succeed, it will be the first time any such pictures have ever been taken. . . . If I don't get hung up on the council, I will bring you in some amazing materials. But I must watch my step—the public relation job is gunpowder." Indeed it was gunpowder. Not only did the pueblo council reject Collier's proposal, but it leaked an account of Collier's plan to rival government agencies and called Stryker on the carpet. He cancelled Collier's plan to photograph Pueblo Indians.

Faced with that rejection, Collier found the subject of his most famous FSA pictures—the Hispanic villages of Peñasco and Las Trampas, New Mexico. His almost daily letters to Stryker in January and February 1943 document how he went about taking them. Throughout America, the FSA founded and helped fund pre-paid single-payer health insurance. The FSA negotiated a fee structure with local physicians and set a premium for FSA clients to pay, sometimes with FSA grants. Collier went to photograph the plan in Peñasco. Doing this led him into an even bigger story when he met the Rev. Walter Cassidy, the Roman Catholic priest serving nearby parishes. He stayed in the home of Juan López, the mayordomo of Las Trampas, even sleeping on the floor of the home. The shoot then proceeded to document the health insurance story, the work of the Church and school, ranch life in the mountains, and daily life in the López home. "Roughly speaking—the story is this," Collier wrote Stryker. "1. The people and the country. 2. The many influences that enter into the modern problem of this particular country. It is a story of 'what is being done!' There is the church and the state, and under this division many subdivisions—the Church, its schools, hospitals, its economic influences . . . even its influences through 'the boy scouts.' Then the state, its schools, its clinic, its conservancy programes of range and forest . . . I have tried in this short time to contact all of these forces and to relate them to the people."[7]

Between his work for the Farm Security Administration and the Fruitland project, Collier worked for Roy Stryker's team of Standard Oil Company photographers. For Standard Oil, Collier shot photographs in Norman Wells of Canada's Northwest Territories (1944) and Colombia (1945). While he was in Colombia, he had a chance to take the photographs in Ecuador that became part of *The Awakening Valley*, a book he did with Ecuadorean anthropologist Anibal Buitron. He also did contract work for *Fortune*, *Ladies Home Journal*, and other magazines.[8]

In an article he wrote on Indian photographer Laura Gilpin, Collier reveals his state of mind and view of his work after his FSA pictures and before those of Fruitland Navajos.[9] Collier truly admired Gilpin's work, but he criticized it in a way that described how he would photograph Indians. Unfortunately for her, Collier wrote, Gilpin (1891–1979) had learned "the pseudo-art conscious soft-focus technique that was the rage of the day, rather than the biting clear images" of Jacob Riis and Lewis Hine. Collier clearly sided with these "two pioneers" and he especially admired "the need for accurate social record [that] produced the sharp negative of Jacob Riis."[10] Collier believed that Gilpin's 1941 book, *The Pueblos*, was "designed as a tourist handbook to the archaeological wonders of New Mexico and Arizona" making "her scenes of Indian life appear more like museum sets than breathing human beings."[11] In contrast, her images on the "home life and agriculture" of modern Mayan Indians that accompanied her post-war book, *Temples in Yucatan*, was "the best objective photography of people that she has yet published."[12] For Collier, the absence of people also plagued her *Rio Grande: River of Destiny*, in which she "chose to almost exclude man from the picture." Collier had longed to see images of "how the men of each [Rio Grande] culture use the waters, how they irrigate their gardens as well as how they pan their gold. And the reader would want to see the harvest of the Rio Grande land, from chili to cotton. Only then would he have a picture of the Rio Grande as a river of destiny."[13] As much as he admired the beauty of Gilpin's images, Collier had clearly developed a different view of photography. Instead of using a traditional view camera as she did, he used the "modern equipment" of the 4 x 5, 35-mm, and Rollei cameras that "make human documentation almost automatic."[14] Instead of photographing landscape, he would concentrate on the lives, work, and play of ordinary people.

As he wrote those words, Collier was already figuring out how to take such pictures of Navajos. In 1948 he and Mary took photographs of Arizona Navajos in Piñon, Wide Ruins, Navajo Mountain, Ganado, Chinle, and Tuba City. For *Farm Quarterly,* they used the photographs to document traditional Navajo life under the impact of World War II and the hardships of the 1947–1948 winter. In doing so, they wrote their first criticism of the stock reduction program of Collier's father. The Navajos found stock reduction "incomprehensible and shocking. They resisted the program one hundred per cent. The Indian Service went ahead with its orders and reduced the herds by force, shooting sheep and goats and dumping the carcasses in trenches. The Indian Service had every intention of balancing the loss in economy. But politics being what they are, most of the planners went on to other jobs. All that remains is the sheep reduction."[15]

Collier's work took a more self-consciously scientific bent when, through his father, he linked up with Alexander H. Leighton.[16] In the 1930s Leighton studied psychiatry with Adolf Meyer at Johns Hopkins University and anthropology with Clyde Kluckhohn of Harvard and Ralph Linton at Columbia University. By 1940 Leighton was in Navajo country. Working with Navajos, Leighton pioneered the use of life histories, the joining of life histories to each other, and the integration of both into a society's culture. The work included such pioneering studies as *Gregorio, the Hand Trembler* (1949). He established the anthropology department of Cornell University as a center for his approach. A major outgrowth was his Cornell University Southwest Project seminar in cross-cultural relations. The seminar used the integration of life histories into a society's culture to compare the Papago, Navajo, and Truchas (New Mexico) Hispanics. Robert Bunker and John Adair describe the seminar's work in their book, *The First Look at Strangers.* John Collier Jr. took the photographs that appear in the book.[17]

In 1948 Leighton began applying his methods of cross-cultural relations to a long-term study of two distinct cultures in the so-called Stirling County Project of adjacent French-speaking and English-speaking farming, fishing, and lumbering communities in Atlantic Canada. Using such techniques as life histories and the mapping of housing, Leighton's study of community development linked the environment to mental health.[18] In 1950 John Collier Jr. joined the project. "This is a long term project and every social move must be made with this in light," he wrote Stryker. "Continuous good will is the prime goal of all project personnel. This slows down picture taking and is a constant consideration that is a decided departure from magazine photography protocol, as you can imagine. Every one was very worried about this but so far my rapport has been excellent and Leighton is a little amazed at how easy it has all been. We run our protocol by the rule, 'trust people and appreciate people and they will trust you.' It really works."[19]

By now, photographing this way came naturally to Collier. As a member of Leighton's team, Collier photographed nearly every dwelling in the county, usually from his car window, to produce a map of socio-economic conditions. Staff anthropologists used his scenes of daily life to conduct interviews. Such photographs were able to "trigger responses that might lie submerged in verbal interviewing." Following Leighton's rule that staff be friendly and unobtrusive, Collier wrote in 1957, "we knew we must conduct ourselves sincerely and openly, and operate on as equal a plane as possible." For his first shoot, he took along his wife and three-year-old son in order to make "the photographic occasion a family visit." Indeed, Mary Collier regularly accompanied him, serving as secretary for the interviews. Collier's deafness may have helped set his subjects at ease. To speak with anyone, he had to get right up next to them, fourteen to eighteen inches from their faces. That intimacy may have established a familiarity that would not otherwise have occurred.[20]

Because of his work at Stirling, Collier was invited to work at Fruitland, New Mexico, with a team of anthropologists led by Tom T. Sasaki. Sasaki's team had chosen Fruitland in 1948 as, to use his book's subtitle, "a Navaho community in transition." It was in transition because Fruitland Navajos were coping with four life-changing events that undermined their lifeways in the fifteen years preceding Collier's arrival in 1952.

The first of these life-changing events was the devastation to sheep raising, the basis of the Navajo economy, by a federal stock reduction program in the 1930s. Theorizing that the Dust Bowl had only worsened the long-term overgrazing of Navajo lands, the Bureau of Indian Affairs, headed by John Collier Sr. (the photographer's father), had decided that the solution to the overgrazing lay in reducing the size of herds. "Rather than reducing individual herds on a percentage basis, . . . stock reduction called for an across-the-board slashing of herds; large owners sacrificed their culls, but the small owners, who formed the vast majority, had the heart cut out of their meager holdings."[21] In cutting in half the herds of sheep and goats, John Collier Sr.'s Bureau slaughtered nearly 400,000 animals in the program's first year, 1934.

A second life-changing event followed the stock reduction. In 1933 the federal government introduced an irrigation project to bring water from the San Juan River to farms around Fruitland. The San Juan, Animas, and La Plata rivers converge at Farmington, New Mexico, a few miles east of the Navajo reservation. Water from that three-river watershed was used to irrigate Navajo farms on the south side of the river and non-Navajo farms on the north side. These water resources have continued to be developed until recent times. Except for the river valley, the land is typical Southwest high desert with altitudes of 5,000 to 6,000 feet, annual rainfall of 6 to 7 inches, and a growing season of under 160 days.[22] By the time Collier took his photographs, a canal on the Navajo side of the river ran from just downstream from the convergence of the three rivers at Farmington to the Hogback, a gigantic sandstone ridge running north and south, eighteen miles downstream. Lateral channels from the canal

Fig. 34

John Collier Jr. in the 1950s at the time of the Fruitland photographs.

Courtesy of Richard W. Brooks.

watered twenty-five hundred acres of Navajo irrigated land on the south side of the San Juan River. A panoramic Collier photograph shows how it worked. In the project's planning stage, Navajos understood that each family would receive twenty acres of irrigated land. In the end, however, each family got only ten-acre plots, not enough for even a subsistence farm. In contrast, non-Navajo farmers held thirty-acre irrigated farms on the north side of the San Juan River upstream to the town of Aztec. Navajos probably had always farmed, but this new farming arrangement was different. To many Navajos, even the two hundred families that held irrigated plots, the irrigation and stock reduction programs seemed to guarantee hardship or starvation. More than that, according to the leader of the Fruitland Project team of anthropologists, the San Juan River irrigation system "forced Navahos into a cash economy."[23]

The third event that changed Navajo life forever was World War II. Navajos, like men and women throughout America, went off to war as servicemen and off-reservation munitions workers. War was a broadening experience for all combatants, but for American Indians especially, the war took them from the self-contained life and culture of their reservation. The war experience, however, was but the beginning of the story. Returning servicemen and munitions workers brought back to the reservation cultural perspectives and skills that Navajo leadership had not had before. Very quickly, Navajo leadership in the new tribal government of chapter houses and tribal council was "modernized."

The fourth life-changing event in the fifteen years before Collier arrived to take his pictures was the discovery of rich oil and gas deposits in the San Juan River basin. The big discoveries occurred in the late 1940s. By the time Collier pitched his family tents in Fruitland, nearly five hundred gas and oil wells were operating. To market the enormous pool of natural gas found in northwestern New Mexico, the El Paso Natural Gas Company had begun a pipeline from Fruitland to California. Several hundred Navajos got jobs in pipeline construction. Their wages caused boom times for Fruitland Navajos and a nearly total change in the way they lived. One study estimates that wage labor increased from 30 percent

Fig. 35

John Collier Jr. took this panorama of the Fruitland project from the mesa top south of the San Juan River. In the distance is the Hogback. The San Juan River runs across the picture just below it. Just below the mesa is the irrigation ditch. The fields watered by the irrigation ditch lie between the ditch and the San Juan River.

Courtesy of Nova Scotia Archives.

Fig. 36

Here is a John Collier Jr. view of the eastern end of the Fruitland Project. The irrigation canal snakes along the bottom of the hill. A dirt road parallels it. The strips of ten or twenty-acre Navajo farms run perpendicular to it toward the San Juan River.

Courtesy of Alexander H. Leighton.

of Navajo income in 1940 to 60 percent of Navajo income in 1960.[24] Taken altogether, the stock reduction program, the irrigation project, returning modernizing veterans and workers, and the new oil and gas business could only disrupt traditional Navajo life and replace much of it with something different.

As part of Tom T. Sasaki's research at Fruitland, John Collier Jr.'s photographs documented these disrupting changes. Sasaki's project had started in the wake of the stock reduction and irrigation projects and the new oil and gas boom. He came as part of Cornell University's Southwest Project, initiated by Alexander H. Leighton. Sasaki, field director of the project from 1952 to 1956, and his team of nineteen social scientists were there to examine the effect of the changes wrought by those four events. They used techniques developed by Leighton. Through open-ended interviews, they collected life histories from individual Navajos and compared them to each other. They attended Navajo celebrations and ceremonies, spent time at trading posts and with government officials, and took notes on what they saw and heard. They also surveyed material wealth to determine Navajo economic and social levels. They used photographs and government records to map this economic and social data. According to Sasaki, these "field methods were devised to secure information on several dimensions: intensive studies of individual personalities and of families and the intercultural contact situation—all in historical and current perspective."[25]

Fruitland Navajos had never seen anthropologists before. As a result, Sasaki's team was initially unwelcome. The team had to convince Navajos that they were not affiliated with the hated Bureau of Indian Affairs or other government agencies, the bringers of the changes disrupting Navajo life. To squelch the widely held Navajo belief that Sasaki, a Japanese-American, was a "spy," the team hired Navajo war veterans as interpreters. Rather than using anthropological jargon, they told Navajos that the team's aim was to see "how the Navaho way of life in the old days compared to that today."[27]

Collier came to Fruitland in 1952 prepared to photograph just such changes. His Stirling experience,

Fig. 37

"Everyone smiled and crowded around to look at this picture," Collier wrote about this *Farm Quarterly* image he showed
Fruitland Navajos in 1952. "She's taking the lambs to the hogan to keep them warm," one Fruitland viewer said.

Courtesy of Nova Scotia Archives.

Fig. 38

Contrast this John Collier Jr. photograph of 1952–1953 with the 1948 image of woman holding lambs. "In the place of sheep," Collier wrote about this image, "Fruitland Navajos have tried to make a living in subsistence farming."

Courtesy of Nova Scotia Archives.

a Carnegie grant, and years at Cornell had made him a social science photographer. Still, the people of Stirling had been part of Collier's own culture. Could Navajos, "with only a scanty exposure to our culture, be able to read the two dimensional patterns of photographs and be able to interpret photographs in an interview?" Starting with his photographs from the *Farm Quarterly,* Collier "assembled an interview file that was designed to gather statements on Navaho life values—general values, not personal statements about personal lives. We also presented a series of panoramic vistas of the Fruitland community itself." The latter did not work very well with "the gossip-wary Navahos. But with the pictures not directly related to themselves and their neighbors," such as the *Farm Quarterly* images, "the interviews were very successful." It turned out that Navajos "were far more fluid [than the people of Stirling] in their photographic reading, giving identification and explanation of fine detail, and being able to state with great accuracy place, season, date and even time of day of a large number of photographs."[27]

This book of John Collier Jr.'s work at Fruitland includes photographs from the *Farm Quarterly* because they were used in that effort. At Fruitland, Collier added to that file images of Fruitland's landscape and homes for the project's mapping. Then he documented the daily life of Fruitland's Navajos for follow-up interviews. Like other photographers, Collier photographed traditional Navajo life—sheep herding, spinning and weaving, meal preparation and dining, and hogan and trading post interiors. But unlike so many photographers of Navajos, his social scientist eye also captured the shift to new Navajo practices and activities—building the El Paso Natural Gas pipeline, plowing, planting, cultivating, and harvesting in the new irrigated farming, and the beginnings of town life for Navajos. In doing this, his photographs came to show the Navajos' shift from being shepherds to agriculturists, from the traditional pastoral Navajo life of raising sheep and weaving wool into Navajo life of increased urbanization, cash-crop agriculture, wage work, and a closer connection to the rest of the world. As a result, he documented a Navajo people different from the Navajo people who were portrayed by earlier photographers.

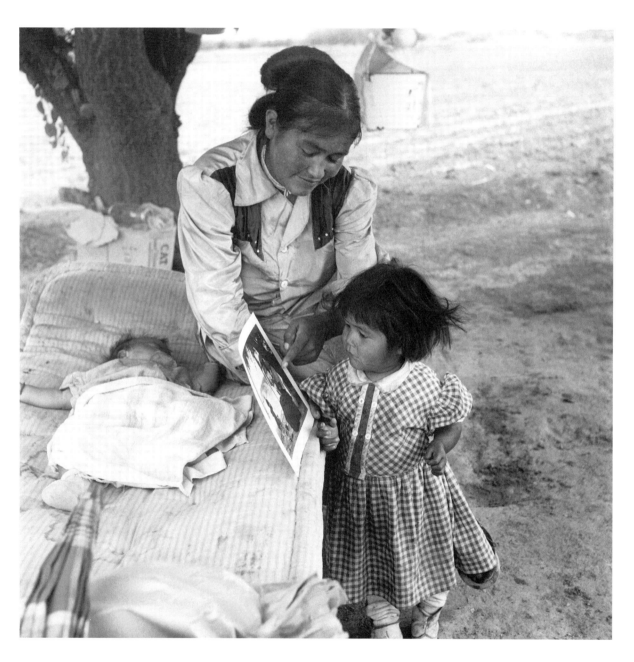

Fig. 39

John Collier Jr. took photographs that interviewers could use to elicit comments from subjects about their lives. Here, Martha Greyhorse shows a picture to her daughter, just as an interviewer might have shown it to her. Her baby is asleep on the mattress. A pot of water hangs in the shade of the tree to keep it cool and away from animals. Summer 1953.

Courtesy of Alexander H. Leighton.

Fig. 40

The Fruitland project anthropologists followed Alexander Leighton's method of making an inventory
of housing. One of John Collier Jr.'s assignments was to take images like this of Fruitland Navajo housing.

Courtesy of Alexander H. Leighton.

Fig. 41

Building a sewer head in a street in Farmington, New Mexico. One of John Collier Jr.'s assignments was to document work in town. "I took the role that the street work was something worth recording. I made long shots of street work." He felt "fast growing Farmington was worth photographing." "I was looking for skills in Navajo work." Summer 1953.

Courtesy of Alexander H. Leighton.

After his work at Fruitland, John Collier Jr. became a professor at San Francisco State University where he was a founder of the field of visual anthropology. Some of his Navajo images appear in the work for which he remains best known—his book *Visual Anthropology,* still in print since its first appearance in 1967 and still the basic handbook for using photographs in anthropology.

Notes

1. John Collier Jr. letter to Roy Stryker, May 25, [1952], in Roy E. Stryker, *Roy Stryker Papers, 1912–1972. Series I: Correspondence, 1924–1972* (Louisville, Ky.: University of Louisville, University Archives & Records Center; Teaneck, N.J.: Exclusive distribution by Chadwyck-Healey, 1978–1981), reel 5 and interview with Mary and Malcolm Collier, April 9, 2001.
2. Seventeen Collier photographs of Papago and Navajo Indians appear in Robert Bunker and John Adair, *The First Look at Strangers* (New Brunswick, N.J.: Rutgers University Press, 1959). Six Collier photographs of Navajos appear in Tom T. Sasaki, *Fruitland, New Mexico: A Navaho Community in Transition* (Ithaca, N.Y.: Cornell University Press, 1960). Seven appear in John Collier Jr. and Malcolm Collier, *Visual Anthropology: Photography as a Research Method* (Albuquerque: University of New Mexico Press, 1986). Eight appear in Mary and John Collier Jr., "Navajo Farm," *Farm Quarterly* 3 (fall, 1948), 16–25 and 103–7. Two appear in James C. Faris, *Navajo and Photography: A Critical History of the Representation of an American People* (Albuquerque: University of New Mexico Press, 1996). The Public Archives of Nova Scotia hold several hundred Collier photographic prints of Navajos. A somewhat different several hundred negatives are held by Alexander H. Leighton, founder of the Cornell Southwest Project in 1948. The University of Pennsylvania holds about sixty Collier photographic prints of Navajos from the *Farm Quarterly* shoot. The Collier family holds many more. Most collections only hold Collier's photographs of 1941–1943 for the Farm Security Administration.
3. John Collier Jr. foreword to Mabel Dodge Luhan, *Edge of the Taos Desert* (Albuquerque: University of New Mexico Press, 1987, c. 1965).
4. Interview with Mary and Malcolm Collier and Roy Stryker letter to Dorothea Lange, December 3, 1941 in reel 3, *Stryker Papers.*
5. John Collier Jr. letter to Roy Stryker from Holyoke, Mass., September 1941 in reel 3, *Stryker Papers.*
6. This paragraph and the next one come from the Collier-Stryker correspondence in reels 3 and 5 of the *Stryker Papers.* Such works as Nancy Wood, *Heartland New Mexico: Photographs of the Farm Security Administration, 1935–1943* (Albuquerque: University of New Mexico Press, 1989) and J. B. Colson, et al, *Far from Main Street: Three Photographers in Depression-Era New Mexico* (Santa Fe: Museum of New Mexico Press, 1994) reproduce the photographs of this assignment.
7. Undated handwritten John Collier Jr. letter to Roy Stryker, reel 5 of the *Stryker Papers.*

8. Interview with Mary and Malcolm Collier and "John Collier Jr. Vita" typescript.

9. John Collier Jr., "Laura Gilpin: Western Photographer," *New Mexico Quarterly* 20 (winter, 1950–1951): 485–93.

10. Ibid., 488.

11. Ibid., 489.

12. Ibid., 490.

13. Ibid., 491–92.

14. Ibid., 487.

15. Mary and John Collier Jr., "Navajo Farm," *Farm Quarterly* 3 (fall, 1948): 16–25 and 103–7.

16. Interviews with Mary and Malcolm Collier, April 9, 2001 and Alexander H. Leighton, July 29, 2000.

17. See Bunker and Adair, *The First Look at Strangers,* passim.

18. The initial study of Stirling County was published as Charles C. Hughes, Marc Adelard Tremblay, Robert Rapoport, and Alexander H. Leighton, *People of the Cove and Woodlot. Communities from the Viewpoint of Social Psychiatry. The Stirling County Study of Psychiatric Disorder and Sociocultural Environment,* vol. 2 (New York: Basic Books, 1960).

19. Collier letter to Roy Stryker, September 22, 1950.

20. John Collier Jr., "Photography in Anthropology: A Report on Two Experiments," *American Anthropologist* 59 (1957): 843–59 and especially 846, 850, and 854 and interviews with Malcolm Collier, Mary Collier, and Alexander Leighton.

21. Peter Iverson, *The Navajo Nation* (Albuquerque: University of New Mexico Press, 1984), 29. For more on John Collier's career and impact on Navajos, see: Lawrence C. Kelly, *The Assault on Assimilation: John Collier and the Origins of Indian Policy Reform.* Foreword by John Collier Jr. (Albuquerque: University of New Mexico Press, 1983) and Kenneth R. Philp, *John Collier's Crusade for Indian Reform, 1920–1954* (Tucson: University of Arizona Press, 1977 and 1981).

22. Sasaki, 4–5.

23. Ibid., 175.

24. Garrick A. Bailey and Roberta G. Bailey, *Historic Navajo Occupation of the Northern Chaco Plateau* (Tulsa, Okla.: Faculty of Anthropology of the University of Tulsa, 1982), 445.

25. Sasaki, xi. Leighton summarizes his techniques in his foreword to Joyce J. Griffen (editor and annotator), *Lucky the Navajo Singer, Recorded by Alexander H. Leighton and Dorothea C. Leighton* (Albuquerque: University of New Mexico Press, 1992).

26. Ibid., xii.

27. John Collier Jr. typescript manuscript notes for an unpublished book, *Stirling County Study, Series D: John Collier Photographs,* Public Archives of Nova Scotia, Halifax. See also Collier letter to Roy Stryker, no date but probably early 1953 and Collier letter to Stryker of April 12, 1952, *Stryker Papers.* For a fuller but later discussion of Fruitland's technique, see Collier, "Photography in Anthropology" and John Collier Jr. and Malcolm Collier, *Visual Anthropology,* rev. ed. (Albuquerque: University of New Mexico Press, 1986), 108–12.

Portfolio:
The Fruitland Project
1952–1953

Wage Work, Town Life

Fig. 42

Navajo workers laying the El Paso Gas Line near Blanco, twenty-five miles east of Farmington. Summer 1953.

Courtesy of Alexander H. Leighton.

Fig. 43

John Collier Jr.'s field notes say that this is the maintenance yard of the El Paso
Gas Co. "where Navajos and white workers gather each morning at 6:30 A.M.
for work on the gas line and production fields." Farmington, summer 1953.

Courtesy of Alexander H. Leighton.

Fig. 44

"That's what we do when we work for El Paso Gas line. That's what they let us do—hold that pipe all day long," a Fruitland Navajo pipeline worker told Collier. Summer 1953.

Courtesy of the Nova Scotia Archives.

Fig. 45

"Saturday afternoon in Farmington," Collier said of this image showing the new urbanization of Fruitland Navajos.

Courtesy of Nova Scotia Archives.

Fig. 46

Another Collier photograph for the Fruitland Project housing inventory.

Courtesy of Nova Scotia Archives.

Fig. 47

Water Flow Trading Post and post office. Rugs for sale hang from the beams and the stove heats the room where customers, like the man seated, gather to socialize.

Courtesy of Alexander H. Leighton.

Fig. 48

Fruitland Navajos outside a brush shade house.

Courtesy of Nova Scotia Archives.

Fig. 49

Jack Cline's Fruitland Trading Post. The shelves are lined with stores
of canned goods and supplies that he traded to Navajo women.

Courtesy of Alexander H. Leighton.

Fig. 50

A Navajo camp sits under the cottonwood trees, on the banks of the San Juan River. Many tents have reinforced wooden sides for insulation in the winter and shade shelters added on for sitting outside in the summer. Farmington 1953.

Courtesy of Alexander H. Leighton.

Fig. 51

Irene Diswood first saw this picture of herself and her children fifty years after it was taken. As she looked at it a friend told her, "There you are, Irene, in your outdoor living room." The children are, left to right, Verlin, Alva, and Retha.

Courtesy of Alexander H. Leighton.

Fig. 52

Sewing on a foot-treadle machine in a one room stone house. Summer 1953.

Courtesy of Alexander H. Leighton.

Fig. 53

Navajos at a fair, with bleachers in the background.

Courtesy of Alexander H. Leighton.

Fig. 55

Jay Yazzie with his wife and two sons. 1952.

Courtesy of Alexander H. Leighton.

Fig. 56

Navajo students in shop class.

Courtesy of Alexander H. Leighton.

Fig. 57

Navajo students in home economics class.

Courtesy of Alexander H. Leighton.

Navajo Farmers in Fruitland, New Mexico, 1952–1953

By Dale Sperry Mudge

MOVING TO NEW FARMING areas was not unusual for Navajo people. Bessie Largo's family had a large 2,000-head sheep farm in Beclabito, west of Shiprock and east of the Carrizo Mountains. Like many sheep farmers they also dry-land farmed. In the 1930s, after the stock reduction, Bessie's father had to change his farming methods to provide for his family. He acquired two large Clydesdale workhorses and moved closer to the wet-land irrigated areas in order to grow legume hay to feed the horses.[1] Irrigated farming was encouraged after the livestock reduction program was enforced. The government set up an incentive program called the Fruitland Project, and Navajos moved to new land to have the opportunity to grow crops and be less dependent on raising livestock.[2] A bargain was struck with one hundred Navajo sheep farmers: they would be relocated from their grazing farms onto twenty acres of irrigated farmland in Fruitland. The farmers were told, "20 acres was the smallest acreage that could be considered as a subsistence farm."[3] But the plan changed to accommodate more families, and relocated farmers never got the twenty acres. They were only allotted ten-acre parcels, which was not sufficient to support their families.[4] Some farmers said, "farms were too small . . . couldn't say how much land they would need but a lot more than this."[5] Being denied the additional promised land was significant for Navajos. They believed "how the land would be used reflected not only economic but cultural and social priorities."[6] Navajo farmers could not grow enough food to support their families—the amount of land allocated meant a subsistence endeavor, not providing a profit—and they had to do off-reservation wage work.[7] Men found ways to supplement their farming, and women had to do the farm work to enable their families to survive. John Collier Jr.'s photographs document the Navajo people's change from traditional farming to creating methods to help supplement their income. By combining Collier's field notes of 1952 with interviews from the spring of 2001 with descendants of the families in Collier's photographs, the farming past of four representative Fruitland Navajo families can be reconstructed.

Navajo farming practices began to change long before Collier arrived in 1952. Around the early 1900s Navajo farmers lived to the north and the south of the San Juan River and later moved when Mormon settlers came to the south shore of the river. The general feeling was "Mormons came in and the Navajos had to leave."[8] The farmland was better on the north side: "on that side is better. . . . That's why the Mormons wanted it!"[9] Although the Mormons displaced Navajo farmers, they brought teams of workhorses and hired Navajo men to help them work and improve their land. These large workhorses were given to Navajo farmers in exchange for wages, and the advantages of acquiring a team changed Navajo farming methods. Many farmers used teams of horses to plow, disc, level, seed, and cultivate the fields. In the fall when the crops were harvested, some farmers would thrash beans and corn by putting them on the ground and beating the bean pods and corncobs with a stick, separating the dried beans from the chaff and the corn kernels from the cobs. Farmers also used their teams to thrash the corn and beans; they dug a long, rectangular, shallow pit in the ground, lined it with a tarp, spread the corncobs or beans in a layer, and walked the team of horses back and forth to thrash. Teams were also used to bring in wagons of hay, corn, and other harvested goods. Workhorses had their advantages but having them required living near irrigated land to insure adequate pasturage.

Prior to the 1930s, the Navajo people still relied on sheep grazing and had not developed crop production for their subsistence. The farms, "they were all small ones—most everybody ran sheep in those days."[10] Navajo farmers in Fruitland "all lived down near the river and they had just one irrigation ditch then, that they had made themselves."[11] "The first ditches were small, and only six or seven family groups had farms."[12] The Mormon farmers helped the Navajos construct larger canals and ditches for the small number of farms.[13] Some Navajo farmers used their teams of horses to haul water from the river, sometimes dragging a wheelbarrow with containers of water up to the farms. Guy Greyhorse remembers his father watering individual plants in the rows by hand, using a small vessel, and pouring the water around each individual plant on ten acres. The irrigation ditch, constructed in 1938–1940, replaced this time-consuming work.[14] The mouth of the ditch originated to the east of Fruitland, feeding from the San Juan River, and flowed west, supplying irrigated water for farms along that portion of the river valley. The water was turned on in late April and flowed all summer until October to insure enough moisture to grow crops. Each farmer was charged one dollar per acre for irrigation and it was the responsibility of each landowner to keep his section clean and free flowing.

In 1950 farming along the flat river basin of the San Juan River consisted of thirty to forty generalized farms.[15] They were laid out in ten-acre tillable plots of land stretched out along the river. Most farmers had just the land that was assigned to them, but some farmers accrued up to fifty acres. With an average of only 156 growing days (sometimes as few as 114 days), and with little land available to work, most of the farms were not self-sufficient. Farms produced crops that provided some of the food for the families and their animals.[16] If there were surplus crops, they were sold to trading posts or

Fig. 58

Willie Pinto thrashing beans with a flail. His wife is piling dried bean pods on the
canvas tarp on the ground. The flail breaks the pods to release beans that fall down onto
the tarp. Afterwards, they place the beans in grain bags for storage. Summer 1952.

Courtesy of Alexander H. Leighton.

Fig. 59

Part of the spring chores was clearing weeds from the ditches feeding off from the
main irrigation ditch. Everyone was responsible for maintaining his or her own ditch.

Courtesy of Alexander H. Leighton.

shared with neighbors and relatives who lived either near the farms or on other parts of the reservation. Some relatives who lived seven miles from Fruitland would walk to help with the farm work in the morning and walk seven miles home in the evening after all of the day's work was completed.[17] Within the neighborhoods, farmers developed a system to share farm work. Not only did neighbors help with the physical farm work, some people who owned pieces of equipment loaned or shared them with other families. Most of the farm jobs were once-a-year operations, like plowing, discing, leveling, or cultivating, and when they were completed, the plow or cultivator was moved from neighbor to neighbor to help prepare the fields for the spring planting. Navajo farmers knew the importance of helping each other and they readily practiced a cooperative effort in farming.

Although most Fruitland Navajo farm families shared many farming practices, they also had unique experiences. Jerry Golbe's family was an example. He had ten acres to support a family of ten. Later he acquired more land and expanded his farm to nineteen acres. The land was divided into a field for an alfalfa hay crop, rotated with corn, an area for fruit trees, and a part for the family vegetable garden. Golbe was a successful and industrious farmer. He built his stone house with the help of his sons by cutting the stones and hauling them down from the mesa behind his land. He also built a root cellar, a "partly subterranean structure, made of well coursed stone, which he said he and his sons chipped and put up."[18] All the family worked hard to provide food for the winter. Golbe's wife, Daisy, canned fruit, vegetables, and meat. Along with the canned goods in the cellar she stored dried mutton, peaches, apples, pumpkins, muskmelons, watermelons, honeydews, cantaloupes, wild celery, and squaw berries for making mush, adding to flour to sweeten baked goods, and as a cereal. The dried goods were tied in bundles to the rafters in the cellar for use all winter. In addition to the chickens and livestock they raised on the farm, they extended their meat supply by eating wild animals. Golbe caught prairie dogs and raised them in a pen to fatten them. He singed the hair over an open fire, dug a hole in the ground,

Fig. 60

Jerry Golbe helping Irene Diswood shell her dried corn, as one of the Golbe daughters watches.
They feed dried corn cobs into the top of the machine and the teeth separate the kernels from the cob.
The separated kernels fall into a pan underneath. Grain bags on the right are filled with apples.

Courtesy of Alexander H. Leighton.

built a fire inside the hole, and then when it was hot, he raked the coals out, and roasted the meat in the ground. They also ate rabbits, venison, porcupines, and locusts.

When families relocated to Fruitland on the allotments, they were not always grouped together. The relocated families had to fit in and join originally settled farm families. The assigned ten-acre sites were given at different times and the traditional way families lived together was no longer feasible. Farmers could no longer utilize help from their large extended families; they had to rely on neighbors to help with the farm jobs. Jerry Golbe helped his neighbors by using his tractor to cut their hay and they in return baled his hay.[19] Before Golbe bought a corn sheller, he shelled his harvested dried corn by taking two corncobs, laden with corn, and rubbing and twisting them together at angles to release the kernels. After Golbe bought a corn sheller, he fed the ends of the dried corncobs into the top and the grinding teeth released the kernels of corn, dropping them out of the bottom. Once his corn was shelled, he shared the corn sheller with his neighbors to help them with their harvest. One person recalled that when she was a child, her mother would give her a twenty-five-pound grain sack that she was allowed to fill with shelled corn. Sometimes it was hard to fill the bag, so she put whole corncobs in the middle to take up the room and sold it at the trading post for $1.05.[20]

In the spring all the neighbors would gather together, using their own teams of horses (sometimes there were four or five teams) with a single plow to plow one field.[21] Then the fields were dragged with logs to level the land. When irrigation started, the dry-farm practice of planting corn in hills was replaced by planting rows, and farmers marked furrows to corrugate for irrigation.[22] Golbe's land was sloping and he had to work hard after the spring run-off to level the field to accept and contain the irrigation.

Wallace Duncan's family had a different set of experiences. Like many Navajos relying on mutual help, the Duncan family practiced a reciprocal exchange of labor with his family from Sanostee, a community east of the Lukachukai Mountains. In 1941 when Duncan got his farm in Fruitland, he selected

Fig. 61

Horses pull a long post with a marker to corrugate rows for irrigation.

Courtesy of Alexander H. Leighton.

ten acres that were farther away from the irrigation ditch because the land was better. Later he was able to get another ten acres, but "even his combined land was not enough to supply the needs of his family." It was necessary for him to work off-reservation on construction jobs, building houses and roads, and as an interpreter. To make ends meet he helped his relatives with their sheep raising and they in turn helped with his crops. That exchange of work provided produce for the family in Sanostee and gave Duncan's family mutton. Duncan felt "farmers usually have some days anyway when there's not too much to do, and it is better to exchange work with somebody else." By exchanging labor a farmer could save money; he wouldn't have to pay someone to help with his work.[23]

When Duncan's relatives took their sheep seven miles to Table Mesa for dipping to kill the parasites on the animals, Duncan's family would make the long trip to help them. Leroy Duncan, Wallace's son, remembers making the two-day trip, camping along the way, to arrive ahead of his father's family at the dipping station. The dip lasted three days and some shepherds had to wait a whole day for their turn. While they waited to have the sheep dipped, they camped and visited with the other families. People from all over the area, some from fifteen miles away, came to the dipping station and waited their turn with their flocks. Leroy and his brothers did not have sheep in Fruitland and, unaccustomed to herding, did not realize the importance of keeping the flock in a contained group. The boys saw the flock of sheep as an opportunity to play and would get in the middle, playing with them and trying to ride them, separating the flock.

At the dipping station everyone stood on both sides of the troughs and the men threw the sheep into vats filled with medicine. The women guided the sheep down the narrow vats with long poles fitted with hooks at the ends. "Ownership of the flocks was vested in the women" and they carefully watched to ensure their sheep did not drown and kept them moving along and into the holding pens.[24] After the sheep were sent through the dipping vats, the family stayed a few days waiting for the sheep to dry. Then Duncan's aunt started her fifteen-mile trip to take the flock up to their sheep camp in the Lukachukai Mountains for the summer. Her family slowly followed and joined her.

In the fall Duncan's relatives, traveling in two or three wagons, made the two-day trip down from the Lukachukai Mountains, southwest of Shiprock, to help him harvest his four acres of corn. The family would work together, staying with Wallace Duncan's family until all the work was done. The men would go into the fields with a wagon and pick the dried corn, and the women would help unload the cobs into a large pile on the ground. Then the women, with the small children at their side, would sit together for days and visit while they shucked the ears of corn.[25] As the corn was shucked it was put into large piles four feet high by twenty feet across separated into blue and white corn. Leroy remembers playing hide-and-seek in the large piles. With his cousins, he would hide and burrow into the corncobs and others would try to find him by stomping around in the corn, trying to bump into an arm or leg.[26]

Wallace Duncan worked his land, leveling it by using a scarifier, a "sort of scoop that picks the dirt up from the high places and can be dumped by using a lever, in the lower places." He then used his horses to pull a large wooden drag to smooth the field. Duncan liked working with teams; he felt they were easier to move on the small plots of land. Plowing was easier with the narrow rows, the horses did not ruin the plants, and the horse-drawn seeder was faster than the hand planter. He also recognized that teams had other advantages. For example, using them was less expensive than maintaining a tractor.[27]

The experience of Guy Greyhorse provides a third example of family farming. He inherited his father's workhorses and land and farmed nineteen acres until the mid-1990s. When Collier photographed the Greyhorse farm, it supported one hundred sheep, twelve cattle, fifty chickens, two pigs, goats, and geese. Greyhorse's farm was in a good location; he had plenty of water, he used the irrigation ditches near his land, and he also had the use of a small spring on the edge of his field, which he enlarged to make a well. He was a productive and successful farmer whose main crops were corn, alfalfa,

Fig. 62

The man at the top of the ramp hurled the sheep down into the vat. The man
with the pole used it "to push the sheep through the vat and to help pull them out if
they looked like they were getting too much water." Edited Collier photo interview.

Courtesy of Nova Scotia Archives.

Fig. 63

Wallace Duncan and his relatives unloading harvested corn from his fields. They raked
the ears off the bed of the wagon into piles for them women to shuck. Fall 1953.

Courtesy of Alexander H. Leighton.

and potatoes. He grew most of the food for his family and sold surplus crops and sheep to the trading post across the river in Waterflow. He intensely farmed his land but found it necessary to work in the winter for wage work and to hire out with his own equipment for wages. When his sister needed her field plowed and was asked if he would charge her he said, "no he was not plowing free . . . she would pay him $4.50 per acre, which is the price he always gets."[28] His farm was more self-contained than other farms. Greyhorse did not exchange labor with extended family. He worked the farm with the help of his immediate family and hired other workers when he needed them. It was generally believed that helpers outside of the family "expected pay as well as food for their labor."[29] He had nine children who helped with the farm work, and his wife also worked to irrigate, plant, hoe, and gather the crops. When Greyhorse was away working, she had to play a larger role in the farming and would sometimes even plow the fields with their tractor. When he was asked if he would rather do wage work than farm, he said he preferred to stay and work on his farm and that he knew how to make money.

During the time Collier photographed the farmers in Fruitland, some of them shared a stationary horse-driven baler. After the hay was cut, they would collect the loose hay in windrows in the fields, and pile it high with pitchforks on horse-drawn wagon beds that were extended with boards. The horse was hooked up to a long pole and walked around and around in a circle to drive the hay bale compressors. Some farmers noticed that the stationary baler was not efficient. Greyhorse explained that horse balers could bale about one hundred bales per day, but with a tractor you could bale three hundred.[30] Balers powered by a horse needed four men to operate, and it took much longer to put up hay than with a tractor-driven baler. Greyhorse could bale all his hay in one day with a tractor. He only had to pay three men six dollars a day, compared with paying four men working more than one day with a horse baler. He was a shrewd farmer who worked his farm efficiently and had a good understanding of how to utilize his time and make his farm productive.

Fig. 64

Hay baling with a horse-driven baler. Collier's Navajo viewer of this photograph said, "this kind of hay-baling—with the horse that goes round and round to operate the hay baler—is an old type operation." It costs "about thirteen cents a bale. The man whose hay is being baled furnished the horse. The man at the far right has to keep going around behind the horse to keep it going. Otherwise, the horse would stop." Collier photo interview.

Courtesy of Nova Scotia Archives.

Willie Pinto's farming experience was different from that of the previous three families. Since Pinto did not inherit his farm, he asked for land from the tribal delegates and they gave him a ten-acre allotment. According to him, the delegates in Window Rock "tried to give it to people who would make good use of it—those who knew how to farm."[31] Pinto moved down from the Lukachukai Mountains and brought his cabin, loaded in four wagons, with him. Pinto knew his "10 A[cres] was not enough for a family to make living on" and he relied on making money by his work as a medicine man. He rode his horse to Carson, a community south of Farmington, to conduct "sings" and practice medicine to supplement his income. Sometimes he stayed a month and returned laden with goods strapped to his horse that people gave him for his work.[32] Pinto and his wife knew he had to make "some money himself outside the farm work . . . otherwise they couldn't make a go of it on what they have."[33]

Since Pinto was older and not able to do heavy farm work, his wife carried out most of the farm responsibilities. She had grown up raising sheep and when they moved down from the mountains to Fruitland she became a good farmer. Their farm produced mostly corn and alfalfa and they also grew beans, squash, watermelons, cherries, peaches, and apricots. The Pintos were proud of their work and Mrs. Pinto worked hard to can the extra produce and dry watermelons and other fruits. The squash was held over until the fall by putting hay on top of it to keep the frost from ruining the crop. They ate mutton, venison, goat, and horsemeat. In hot weather she cooked meals outside on a wire-legged grill, making fried corn with hot chiles, frying squash blossoms, and making fry bread.

The Fruitland landscape has changed since Collier's 1952–1953 photographs. Now, driving along the river, you notice the cottonwood trees are larger, fields are divided into more farms, and there are many more houses. It is hard to identify the original farms and difficult to imagine the Navajo farmers' lives during those years. Collier's photographs remind us of how farmers worked at that time. The changes you see today started with the beginning of a "boom" time in the 1950s when wage work

Fig. 65

Medicine man Willie Pinto, surrounded by some of his possessions, poses
in the addition to his log house that he built from scrap lumber. Fall 1952.

Courtesy of Alexander H. Leighton.

opened up in the El Paso Natural Gas Company and Navajo men were hired to work on the railroads.[34] Those opportunities for employment meant that farming became less and less important for family survival. Collier's photographs also documented the new wage workplace.

John Collier Jr. may have documented the farm work, but he could not make images of the individual struggles and experiences of trying to live on the inadequate acreage. Most people farmed and also worked away for wages and that meant that all family members had to pitch in to help. Collier took pictures of men doing farm work and included some photographs of women working alongside them. The field notes describe his reluctance to photograph women and their shyness toward him. Despite his awareness, from looking at the photographs of women helping farm it appears that he was successful in making them comfortable. You wonder if his images tell only part of the story. The interviews describe women who shared the responsibility of the farming and were successful at it.

For the many farmers who did not have access to grazing land and could not raise sheep, some felt sheep farmers had a better situation. Sheep farmers could choose to use the sheep as collateral toward goods they wanted from the trading posts. A trader, knowing that in the spring wool and lambs would be brought to them for sale, would loan money against that commodity.[35]

Today, the workhorses are gone, and although you might see horse-drawn equipment in the yards, it is not used. People living on these lands are part-time farmers, and farming now consists of growing an alfalfa hay crop and corn for individual use and perhaps some for commercial sale. Many families still put in vegetable gardens for fresh produce. The Navajo people still hold land in high regard and feel a strong connection to the privilege of having a farm. The purpose of farming has changed; many people in Fruitland work their land so they can keep their farm permits, allowing them to keep the land that has been passed down from generation to generation.[36] They farm not to provide for themselves; they farm to maintain a lifestyle.

Notes

1. Bessie Largo, personal interview, April 2001.

2. Tom T. Sasaki, *Fruitland New Mexico: A Navaho Community in Transition* (Ithaca, N.Y.: Cornell University Press, 1960), 36.

3. Peter Iverson, *The Navajo Nation* (Albuquerque: University of New Mexico Press, 1984), 35.

4. Sasaki, *Fruitland New Mexico,*12.

5. John Collier Jr. 1952–1953, field notes in the Dorothea C. Leighton and Alexander H. Leighton Collection, Cline Library, Northern Arizona University Library, Flagstaff, Ariz. 1st photo interview, Guy Greyhorse, 9 July 1953, 3.

6. Peter Iverson, "We Are Still Here," *American Indians in the Twentieth Century, The American History Series* (Wheeling, Ill.: Harlan Davidson, Inc., 1998), 3.

7. Garrick A. Bailey and Roberta G. Bailey, *Historic Navajo Occupation of the Northern Chaco Plateau* (Tulsa, Okla.: Faculty of Anthropology of the University of Tulsa, 1982), 480.

8. John Collier Jr. 1952–1953, field notes in the Dorothea C. Leighton and Alexander H. Leighton Collection, Cline Library, Northern Arizona University Library, Flagstaff, Ariz. 4th photo interview, Guy Greyhorse, 30 July 1953, 1.

9. Ibid., 1.

10. Ibid., 5.

11. John Collier Jr. 1952–1953, field notes in the Dorothea C. Leighton and Alexander H. Leighton Collection, Cline Library, Northern Arizona University Library, Flagstaff, Ariz. 3rd non-photo interview, Willie Pinto, 22 July 1953, 5.

12. Ibid., 5.

13. Sasaki, *Fruitland New Mexico,* 21.

14. Ibid., 11.

15. Ibid., 6.

16. Ibid., 4.

17. Jay Yazzie, personal interview, April 2001.

18. John Collier Jr. 1952–1953, field notes in the Dorothea C. Leighton and Alexander H. Leighton Collection, Cline Library, Northern Arizona University Library, Flagstaff, Ariz. 1st non-photo interview, Jerry Golbe, 26 July 1953, 2.

19. John Collier Jr. 1952–1953, field notes in the Dorothea C. Leighton and Alexander H. Leighton Collection, Cline Library, Northern Arizona University Library, Flagstaff, Ariz. 1st non-photo interview, Jerry Golbe, 26 July 1953, 6.

20. Irene Nez, personal interview, May 2001.

21. Richard Golbe, personal interview, February 2001.

22. Sasaki, *Fruitland New Mexico,* 25.

23. John Collier Jr. 1952–1953, field notes in the Dorothea C. Leighton and Alexander H. Leighton Collection, Cline Library, Northern Arizona University Library, Flagstaff, Ariz. 1st non-photo interview, Wallace Duncan, 5 July 1953, 2.

24. Iverson, "We Are Still Here," 43; and passim for more discussion of the empowerment of women, and of women and their sheep.

25. Leroy Duncan, personal interview, April 2001.

26. Leroy Duncan, personal interview, May 2001.

27. John Collier Jr. 1952–1953, field notes in the Dorothea C. Leighton and Alexander H. Leighton Collection, Cline Library, Northern Arizona University Library, Flagstaff, Ariz. 1st non-photo interview, Wallace Duncan, 5 July 1953, 3.

28. John Collier Jr. 1952–1953, field notes in the Dorothea C. Leighton and Alexander H. Leighton Collection, Cline Library, Northern Arizona University Library, Flagstaff, Ariz. 2nd photo interview, Guy Greyhorse, 13 July 1953, 5.

29. Sasaki, *Fruitland New Mexico,* 23.

30. John Collier Jr. 1952–1953, field notes in the Dorothea C. Leighton and Alexander H. Leighton Collection, Cline Library, Northern Arizona University Library, Flagstaff, Ariz. 1st photo interview, Guy Greyhorse, 9 July 1953, 5.

31. John Collier Jr. 1952–1953, field notes in the Dorothea C. Leighton and Alexander H. Leighton Collection, Cline Library, Northern Arizona University Library, Flagstaff, Ariz. 2nd non-photo interview, Mrs. Willie Pinto, 16 July 1953, 2.

32. Ethel and Ruben Yazzie, personal interview, June 2001.

33. John Collier Jr. 1952–1953, field notes in the Dorothea C. Leighton and Alexander H. Leighton Collection, Cline Library, Northern Arizona University Library, Flagstaff, Ariz. 2nd non-photo interview, Mrs. Willie Pinto, 16 July 1953, 3.

34. Bailey and Bailey, *Historic Navajo Occupation,* 466.

35. Irene Nez, personal interview, May 2001.

36. Joanne Benally, personal interview, June 2001.

Portfolio:
The Fruitland Project
1952–1953

Four Farming Families

Fig. 66

Wallace Duncan's relative harvesting corn with the team of horses, Bessie and Slim. She and her helpers took about one and one-half hours to gather a wagon load of ripe ears. After they finished the harvesting, they brought back the corn and put it in large piles to be shucked by the women. Fall 1953.

Courtesy of Alexander H. Leighton.

Fig. 67

Wallace Duncan and relatives return from a morning of harvesting corn. Everyone is seated
on the top of the load. A large pile of brightly colored corn is on the ground to the right.

Courtesy of Alexander H. Leighton.

Fig. 68

Wallace Duncan's family shucking corn. Piles, separated
into colors, are twenty feet across by four feet deep. Fall 1953.

Courtesy of Alexander H. Leighton.

Fig. 69

Wallace Duncan's family and relatives from Sanostee, New Mexico, eat lunch after a morning harvesting corn.
A tarp is spread out for the pots of mutton broth, mutton stew, tortillas, and coffee to be shared. The wood
cook stove in the background heats the cabin and cooks the meals. Often Collier would bring his family
to photographic shoots. Malcolm Collier, John Collier Jr.'s son, is in the middle of the picture. Fall 1953.

Courtesy of Alexander H. Leighton.

Fig. 70

Wallace Duncan's sister-in-law, Rosalind, weaving at her sheep camp in the Lukachukai Mountains. In the Canada Dry box, she stores carded rovings waiting to be spun into yarn. She sits on flour sacks sewn together and spread on the ground to keep the rug clean from the forest debris. Summer 1953.

Courtesy of Alexander H. Leighton.

Fig. 71

Sweathouse near Wallace Duncan's relatives' sheep camp in the Lukachukai Mountains. Summer 1953.

Courtesy of Alexander H. Leighton.

Fig. 72

"Sheep were driven 15 miles or more from isolated ranges, so Navajos came prepared to stay"
at this camp near the sheep dip on Table Mesa, commented a sheep farmer to John Collier Jr.
They "camped just long enough near vats to get their sheep taken care of." It was a "time for fun
when the work was over and there was usually a lot of visiting." Some Navajos walked with
the sheep; others drove them with horses and relatives farther away joined them with their trucks.

Courtesy of Nova Scotia Archives.

Fig. 73

The beginning of a sheep dip, "driving the sheep up to put them in a lane leading to the vat."
Flocks wait in the background for their turn at the dip. Edited Collier photo interview.

Courtesy of Nova Scotia Archives.

Fig. 74

Traditional and modern dressed Navajo women, an interviewee told John Collier Jr., "were standing on either side of the vat with their poles pushing the sheep along, pushing their heads under water, and ready to pull one up if he started to drown."

Courtesy of Nova Scotia Archives.

Fig. 75

This was the end of the vat where they took the sheep out. According to one of Collier's informants, it had "always been the women's job he guessed to see that the sheep got out of the water." The women "get excited and think these sheep are not going to get out and they think they have to pull them out." The sheep belonged to the women. When all the sheep had been dipped, they were counted. The job had cost five cents per sheep.

Courtesy of Nova Scotia Archives.

Fig. 76

The Jerry Golbe family sits in the shade of the Chinese Elm in their yard. In the back row, left to right, are Robert, Richard, Jerry, Daisy, Jerry (with Darlene on his lap), and Maxine. In the front row, left to right, are Charlotte, Mary, and Betty. Woven shawls make the backdrop. Daisy's sister, Mary Casey, wove the rug that is on the ground. Fall 1952.

Courtesy of Alexander H. Leighton.

Fig. 77

Guy Greyhorse planting beans. Collier said, "Guy appeared to be skilled with machinery and took great pains to grease all the working parts of the planter, and thoroughly tested the machinery before hitching up the team. Once he started planting he worked without stopping, pausing just long enough to check to see if the drill was depositing the seeds in the ground." Summer 1953.

Courtesy of Alexander H. Leighton.

Fig. 78

According to John Collier Jr., "Mrs. Greyhorse took a great interest in the planting, and when Mr. G. stopped to check, she joined him and helped look for the buried beans." Collier observed that Guy was not self-conscious about being photographed working. Rather, he seemed to have just one thought, "to plant beans." July 8, 1953.

Courtesy of Alexander H. Leighton.

Fig. 79

Pieces of raw wool fleece on a grain bag in the sun with white chalk-like, possibly gypsum rocks to bleach. Some Navajos say that the rocks come from the Bisti area, south of Farmington. Greyhorse farm, summer 1953.

Courtesy of Alexander H. Leighton.

Fig. 80

Elsie Greyhorse weaving. She displays a Navajo wedding basket on the wall. Fall 1953.

Courtesy of Alexander H. Leighton.

Fig. 81

Medicine man and farmer Willie Pinto poses inside his log cabin that he moved down in wagons from the Lukachukai Mountains. When Collier took the photograph he commented, "Willie loves company." Fall 1952.

Courtesy of Alexander H. Leighton.

Fig. 82

Willie Pinto in his melon patch. Summer 1952.

Courtesy of Alexander H. Leighton.

Fig. 83

Willie Pinto painting a sandpainting design with watercolors. His two sons watch him.
He displays a silver concho and beaded belt on the table. Winter 1952.

Courtesy of Alexander H. Leighton.

Fig. 84

Gourds drying in the sun for winter use.

Courtesy of Nova Scotia Archives.

Fig. 85

According to Collier, tractors were used for cultivating
government-developed fields in an experimental farm. 1952.

Courtesy of Alexander H. Leighton.

Fig. 86

John Collier's field notes say that the sheep was hoisted to a post in the crook of a tree, where it was gutted and butchered. "She did all the butchering of the sheep while the rest of us watched. She had bought it for $20 from a friend and considered it a bargain." Summer 1953.

Courtesy of Alexander H. Leighton.

Fig. 87

In preparation for planting, Navajos plow the fields and drag a spring-tooth
harrow over the furrows to break apart lumps of soil. Summer 1953.

Courtesy of Alexander H. Leighton.

Fig. 88

At first, Fruitland Navajos tried to grow corn on their irrigated
plots. Later they turned to growing alfalfa as a cash crop.

Courtesy of Nova Scotia Archives.

Fig. 89

The Fruitland Navajo family is weeding onions. The mother
is harvesting corn. The pet fawn is pestering the little boy.

Courtesy of Nova Scotia Archives.

Fig. 90

Putting up hay. Laying boards down extended the wagon beds for loading loose hay. Fall 1953.

Courtesy of Alexander H. Leighton.

Fig. 91

Navajo women gathering eggs.

Courtesy of Nova Scotia Archives.

Fig. 92

Rows of corn with the Hogback in the distance. Navajos originally planted corn, their traditional crop. Extension workers advised against corn, favoring alfalfa as a needed soil builder. Summer 1952.

Courtesy of Alexander H. Leighton.

Fig. 93

A government corral, where stock was annually branded and counted
in compliance with federal grazing regulations. Summer 1952.

Courtesy of Alexander H. Leighton.

Fig. 94

Melons stored under alfalfa hay, to protect them from early frosts.
Sometimes melons were dried and stored for winter use. Summer 1952.

Courtesy of Alexander H. Leighton.

Fig. 95

A Navajo woman standing next to her canning. Summer 1952.

Courtesy of Alexander H. Leighton.

Fig. 96

Fruitland family harvesting.

Courtesy of Nova Scotia Archives.

Fig. 97

Planting corn using a digging stick. A hole was dug and a handful of corn was dropped inside. When
Collier asked someone about the picture he said, "They don't know anyone who plants that way today,
old people used to use it, too hard and slow." Before machinery, this hill planting method was used.
Some felt that it was better than plowing and harrowing first because you didn't expose the soil to erosion
and when the stalks grew in a clump they supported each other so the wind wouldn't blow them down.

Courtesy of Alexander H. Leighton.

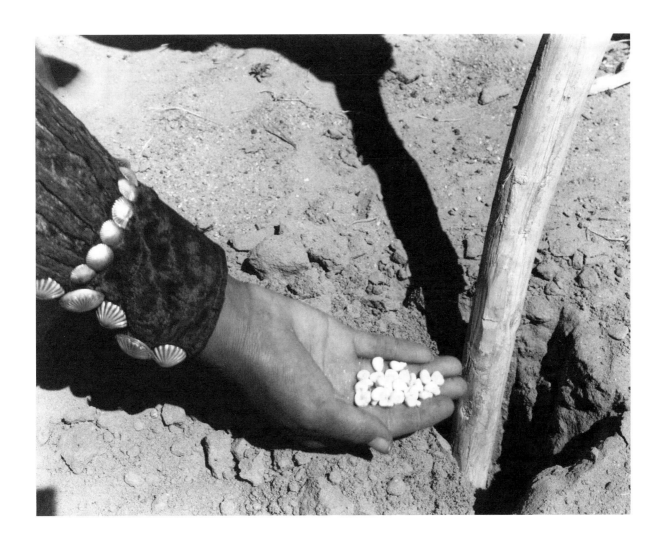

List of Photographs